The Power of Branding

CORWIN
CONNECTED
EDUCATORS
SERIES

The Power of Branding

Telling Your School's Story

Tony Sinanis
@TonySinanis

Joseph Sanfelippo
@Joesanfelippofc

CORWIN
A SAGE Company

CORWIN
A SAGE Company

FOR INFORMATION:

Corwin

A SAGE Company

2455 Teller Road

Thousand Oaks, California 91320

(800) 233-9936

www.corwin.com

SAGE Publications Ltd.

1 Oliver's Yard

55 City Road

London EC1Y 1SP

United Kingdom

SAGE Publications India Pvt. Ltd.

B 1/I 1 Mohan Cooperative Industrial Area

Mathura Road, New Delhi 110 044

India

SAGE Publications Asia-Pacific Pte. Ltd.

3 Church Street

#10-04 Samsung Hub

Singapore 049483

Printed in the United States of America

A catalog record of this book is available from the Library of Congress.

ISBN 978-1-4833-7191-7

This book is printed on acid-free paper.

Executive Editor: Arnis Burvikovs

Associate Editor: Ariel Price

Editorial Assistant: Andrew Olson

Production Editor: Amy Schroller

Copy Editor: Janet Ford

Typesetter: C&M Digitals (P) Ltd.

Proofreader: Dennis W. Webb

Cover and Interior Designer: Janet Kiesel

Marketing Manager: Lisa Lysne

Certified Chain of Custody
SUSTAINABLE FORESTRY INITIATIVE
Promoting Sustainable Forestry
www.sfiprogram.org
SFI-01268
SFI label applies to text stock

14 15 16 17 18 10 9 8 7 6 5 4 3 2 1

Contents

Preface

Welcome to the Connected Educators Series.

The past few years have provided momentous changes for educators: Whether it's the implementation of the Common Core State Standards, educational innovations due to technology, teacher and administrator evaluations, or budget cuts, what is clear is that educational reforms come in different shapes and sizes. For many connected educators, one of the invaluable group support systems essential during these times is the professional learning network, also known as our PLN.

Our PLN can provide innovative ideas, current resources, and sound educational practices that stretch our thinking in ways we haven't yet experienced. Equally as important as how a PLN can professionally expand our horizons, it introduces new friends that we look forward to meeting in person. This Connected Educators Series brings together some important members of my PLN. These are educators with a depth of knowledge and level of experience that help me stay current and up-to-date with my educational practices.

In this series, my book, *Flipping Leadership Doesn't Mean Reinventing the Wheel*, takes the innovative idea of flipping classrooms and presents it at the school leader level, engaging the school community in new and innovative ways. In *Connected Leadership*, Spike Cook shares his experiences moving from a novice to digital leadership and illustrates how other educators can do the same.

Digital experts Tom Whitby and Steven Anderson help increase your digital experience by using Twitter to locate a PLN to engage in daily professional development. In *The Relevant Educator,* Tom and Steve provide a plethora of tools to use and define each and every one. Using those same tools, in their book *The Power of Branding,* Tony Sinanis and Joe Sanfelippo help you to brand your school in order to create a positive focus on the learning happening within the four walls. In his book, *All Hands on Deck,* Brad Currie offers us ways to engage with families and students using old techniques with new innovative approaches.

In *Teaching the iStudent,* Mark Barnes provides insight into the life and mind of the iStudent, and in *Empowered Schools, Empowered Students,* Pernille Ripp focuses on empowering students and teachers. Also in the series, in *Missing Voices of EdTech Conversations,* Rafranz Davis shows how equity and diversity are vital to the social media movement and why they are so important to education as we move forward.

Kristen Swanson from the Edcamp Foundation not only focuses on why the Edcamp model is a new innovative way to provide excellent professional development, but she also explains how you can create an Edcamp in your school district in *The Edcamp Model: Powering Up Professional Learning.*

The books in the Connected Educators Series are designed to read in any order, and each provides information on the tools that will keep us current in the digital age. We also look forward to continuing the series with more books from experts on connectedness.

As Michael Fullan has said for many years, technology is not the right driver, good pedagogy is. The books in this connected series focus on practices that lead to good pedagogy in our digital age. To assist readers in their connected experience, we created the Corwin Connected Educators companion website (www.corwin.com/connectededucators) where readers can connect with the authors and find resources to help further their experience. It is our hope and intent to meet you where you are in your digital journey and elevate you as educators to the next level.

Peter M. DeWitt, Ed.D. @PeterMDeWitt

About the Authors

Tony Sinanis is in his seventh year as the Lead Learner of Cantiague Elementary School in Jericho, New York. Cantiague was named a 2012 National Blue Ribbon School, and Tony received the 2014 New York State Elementary Principal of the Year Award and the national 2013 Bammy Award for Elementary School Principal of the Year. Tony taught at the elementary level for eight years and graduated from New York University with a degree in Early Childhood and Elementary Education and then went on to receive his master's degree in Educational Technology and an advanced certificate in Educational Leadership and Technology from the New York Institute of Technology. Tony is currently enrolled in a doctoral program at the University of Pennsylvania where he is studying the relationship between active participation on *Twitter* and the professional development of principals. Tony is active on Twitter (@TonySinanis), serves as the founder and comoderator of #NYedchat and comoderator of #PTChat, and has presented at both national and local conferences on his work with social media and school branding. Finally, Tony cohosts the BrandED radio show with Dr. Sanfelippo; the show has been rated as high as number #5 on iTunes.

Joe Sanfelippo is currently in his fourth year as the superintendent of the Fall Creek School District in Fall Creek, Wisconsin. Joe holds a BA in Elementary and Early Childhood Education from St. Norbert College, a MS in Educational Psychology from the University of Wisconsin-Milwaukee, an MS in Educational Leadership, and a PhD in Leadership, Learning, and Service from Cardinal Stritch University. Joe was an elementary teacher, school counselor, and elementary principal before taking on the superintendent role. He cohosts the BrandED Radio Show on the Bam Radio Network. Joe serves on the Wisconsin Educator Effectiveness Teachscape Team developed by the Department of Public Instruction (DPI). His research interests include: organizational and systems change in schools; personalized professional growth for staff; and advancing the use of social media in school districts. Joe can be found online through his website at www.jsanfelippo.com and on Twitter at @joesanfelippofc. Go Crickets!

Introduction

In a time when discussions about education are dominated by standards, high-stakes testing, increased budget cuts, and educator evaluation systems, we believe the time has come for educators to refocus the lens on what matters most—students and learning! How do we accomplish this goal? We use our voices to tell our collective stories so that we can flatten the walls of our buildings and brand the experiences unfolding in our schools. We are taking control of the perception the community has about how we instruct children and are sharing stories, e-mails, images, captions, blog posts, and videos that spotlight much of the teaching and learning that is unfolding in our schools and districts. Just to be clear, we are Joseph Sanfelippo, superintendent in Fall Creek, Wisconsin, and Tony Sinanis, lead learner of Cantiague Elementary School in Jericho, New York.

While flattening the walls of the school is a priority, making certain that the brand is transparent to the members within the organization is critical—we must all be telling the same story that we believe in and can stand behind. Work needs to be done during faculty gatherings, informal conversations, and various meetings to ensure that the brand is transparent to the entire team within the organization. This is imperative if we are going to effectively sell the brand outside of the school and ensure that the brand promise matches the brand experience, which is the most important component for our students. The possibilities for how schools and districts go about telling their stories are endless; in this book we explore the importance of telling our stories, the necessity to build our school/district brands, the role that social media can play in branding, and the tools and resources to use to bring the stories to life. The time has come for educators, students, and families to use their voices, take control of their stories, and begin thinking about how a school or district community can brand their space. Branding is defined as the marketing practice of creating a name, symbol, or design that identifies and differentiates a product from other products. Stop and close your eyes for a minute and picture the Golden Arches, or the Nike swoosh symbol, or the Apple on many of your devices—those logos cause people to react, reflect, and even evoke specific feelings and emotions. All that from a simple logo. Well, that is the power of branding. That is why telling the story of our districts, schools, or classrooms is a must—we want the community to know what is happening, and we want them to feel a certain way about what is happening. We can control these reactions by devoting time to branding our spaces and telling our stories.

As you prepare to dive into this book and begin thinking about how you can brand your space and tell your story, we offer the following guiding questions to anchor your thinking and planning:

- Does the brand promise of your school or district match your own brand experience?
- What is your story? What do you believe in? What do you stand for? What do you want for your students and staff?
- If your staff was asked the questions above, would they answer them the same way that you did?
- If your students were asked the questions above, would their responses match your answers?
- If your community was asked the above questions, would they answer in the same way?

Although the target audience for this book is the educational leader, we do believe any and all educators can benefit from interacting with this text. We all have a story to tell and instead of allowing others to tell the story based on secondhand information or misperceptions, we need to devote time to this important aspect of our professions—creating a brand and telling a story—our stories. This book explains why branding is important in this day and age, offers concrete suggestions and tips on how to begin branding your space, and outlines different platforms and tools to use to tell your story. We spotlight various digital tools and resources that can serve as a catalyst for building your brand and sharing your story.

The Importance of Telling Your Story

W hen is the last time something amazing happened in your classroom? I'll help you out . . . the last time you had kids in your classroom and they were engaged in learning, it was awesome. To think that there are people in this world with the skill level to engage a group of children of varying abilities, backgrounds, races, needs, and interests is extraordinary. The work done in schools all across the world is spectacular. Kids gather . . . learn . . . leave . . . and make the world we live in a better place. So, . . . *amazing* happens all the time.

As lead learners, administrators, and educators, it is our responsibility to transform the thick brick barriers surrounding our school buildings into clear, transparent walls of glass! We should want our community to see all the amazing things happening in school, and we should want our children to have a strong connection with the community around them. A positive and productive home/school connection rooted in strong two-way communication is critical to the success of all students and schools. In this day and age of Common Core standards, educator evaluations, value-added measures, and the high-stakes testing craze that consumes our schools, we cannot lose sight of what matters most and why we entered the world of education—to make a difference in the lives of children. Together, with the families of our students, we must collaborate to help our children learn, grow, and develop the skills they need to become successful adults who contribute positively to the world!

Based on our various conversations with numerous other educators from across the country, communications between home and school seem to be inconsistent—at best. In some cases, parents get a monthly newsletter, which is fine except it is hard to talk to your child about something they did weeks ago. In other settings, parents have to rely on interrogating their child to find out a little bit about what is happening in school. Are we letting others tell our story through monthly, or even less frequently distributed, newsletters or fragmented communications with families? We really don't understand how this is possible in 2014 when telling our stories and branding our schools should receive the highest priority and is a story that we can accomplish through so many different means, resources, and platforms!

So, we have a few questions for you . . . think about them carefully because they will serve as the foundation for this journey. Why do we work so hard to keep everything hidden in our classrooms and in our schools? Why not share all of the amazing things happening in our spaces with the parents and community? Why not spotlight the successes (and challenges) that our children are experiencing each day at school? As parents and family members, we want nothing more than to know what our children are learning about in school and how they feel about their learning experiences and about themselves as learners. As educators, one of the highlights of our day is sharing all of the awesome learning and teaching happening in our spaces—whether through an e-mail to parents, tweets throughout the day, or a blog post, we want the entire community to know that incredible things are happening in our school every minute of the day. Why? So, we can begin branding our school and telling our story!

> We want to ensure that OUR voices are the ones telling OUR story—we cannot let anyone else tell our story for us!

The idea of branding schools isn't about selling kids or making false promises; it's about promoting the amazing things happening in our schools for those who don't have the opportunity to experience them on a daily basis. The percentage of people in your community who have kids in schools is relatively small. Only 20 to 30 percent of our communities are made up of households with students in our buildings. Those percentages reflect the huge void of people in the community who have any knowledge of what goes on in your school building. Telling the story of the wonderful things happening in schools to the kids who see it all the time is simply not enough. Students understand the experience because they live it . . . we need to make connections to everyone else because the 70 to 80 percent can serve as an incredible asset to the 20 to 30 percent who walk through the hallways. That large percentage is the group that normally tells the stories of their community and their experiences with the school system. Schools have the opportunity to define their space, provide an identity to those who live within their boundaries, and become a model for communities to support. Some community members come to you . . . they show up at games, concerts, school plays . . . and when they do, the performances on courts, fields, and stages is only part of the story. The feeling they have when they leave your building is the one that gets talked about at dinner tables, local restaurants, and at work the next day. Conversely, other community members do not participate, but if both community segments are speaking the same language and identify with your brand it helps build a great deal of social capital to celebrate the wonderful work of kids. These efforts shape perception and inform reality!

As we consider the power of perception informing reality, let's take a look at Tony's transition from classroom teacher to building administrator.

"People's perception becomes their reality and so we must shape the perception to create the reality we want people to have when they think of us." My superintendent, who hired me for my first administrative position, used to say this to me on a daily basis. Initially it was rooted in the fact that I didn't necessarily wear a suit or shirt and tie each day to school and he felt strongly that the way I looked shaped the way people viewed me and interacted with me. They had a perception of me that spread through word of mouth and thus became the reality. I was still relatively young at the time and would always fight back because I argued it shouldn't matter what I looked like, but instead my words and actions should matter. Eventually I started to think about the perceptions I created solely based on the way someone looked and I realized the only way I was going to get people to hear my words and attend to my actions was by creating a certain perception (that may or may not have been related to my appearance) and in turn my reality.

This idea came back to me about a year ago when I heard Eric Sheninger (@NMHS_Principal) speak about using the power of social media to tell our story and "brand" our schools. Brilliant— absolutely brilliant! Think of the Golden Arches—everyone knows about McDonalds and what a deal it is to eat there. Think about Apple—everyone knows they are always looking for the next iPhone or iPad—they are innovators and risk takers! Last summer I was in Aruba and they have branded themselves as "One Happy Island." You know what? EVERYONE perceives this place as one happy island. Branding is key. Telling our stories is key. Eric was 100 percent right, and I knew that I had to get behind the idea and tell our story—I wanted to influence the perception of our school by sharing the daily realities. I wanted to help brand Cantiague Elementary School as the best elementary school on the planet. Why should we allow people to create their own perceptions, which are often rooted in misinformation, based on word of mouth, or whatever is published in the local paper?

Branding, which typically is a "business world" term, is exactly what our schools need today. There is so much bashing of public education in the media today, and the landscape of public education is not a pretty one, but as educators (superintendents, classroom teachers, support specialists, or the lead learners of the building), we still control most of what happens in our schools. And since we control what happens in our schools (even with state and federal mandates and policies, the final execution is our call), and we know that there are awesome techniques, approaches, and programs unfolding in our schools, let's spread the word; let's brand our schools; let's fuel the perceptions; and let's create our realities.

In case you don't believe that branding and telling your story are important, let's look at some of the research that exists related to the power of branding. When schools, families, and community groups work together to support learning, children tend to do better in school, stay in school longer, and like school more. Furthermore, when schools build partnerships with families that respond to their concerns and honor their contributions, they are successful in sustaining connections aimed at improving student achievement (Henderson & Mapp, 2002). We know that by telling our story, we engage our communities on a whole different level. As spotlighted above, when communities are engaged and connected, we see a positive impact on student achievement.

 CHAPTER 1—TWO TAKEAWAYS & A TIP

- Takeaway #1—The idea of branding schools isn't about marketing kids or making false promises . . . it's about promoting the amazing things happening for those who don't have the opportunity to experience them on a daily basis.

- Takeaway #2—As lead learners, administrators, and educators, it is our responsibility to transform the thick brick barriers surrounding our school buildings into clear, transparent walls of glass!

- Tip—We know there are awesome techniques, approaches, and programs unfolding in our schools, so let's spread the word and start branding our schools. Decide on the platform, resource, or tool you want to use to tell your story and start shouting it from the rooftops!

Your Heart = Your Story

From the moment our own children were born, our goals as educators began to evolve, grow, and expand. We instantly wanted to do whatever we could to keep our children safe, happy, and fulfilled on every level. Initially, it was difficult to see how this unconditional love for our own children would manifest itself in our classrooms and schools, and how it would shape us as educators. However, within weeks it was clear that our parental love quickly molded us, impacted us, and became the anchor for our methodologies as Lead Learners . . . we became leaders with heart! From very early on in our careers, it was our goal to keep our students safe, happy, and fulfilled on every level. It was our objective to keep our staffs safe, happy, and fulfilled on every level. It was our mission to blend all the theoretical stuff we learned in "educational administration school" with what we knew made sense to us. Yes, being logical, practical, and rational were all critical keys to our success as lead learners (i.e., putting out those fires, responding to the multitude of e-mails, managing the budget, etc.), but without adding heart and love to the mix, our successes as educational communities would be nonexistent.

Although branding one's space relies heavily on matters of the mind, without a direct connection to the heart and soul of the organization, there is no real story to tell. The stories become superficial and only touch the surface. When we consider the stories we want to tell about our spaces, we know that they are rooted in a common vision and collective effort to do what is best for our entire community. A school vision starts at the core; the vision starts in the space that makes the organization tick; the vision starts in the traditions and values of the organization; the vision starts in the space that makes the organization breathe and come to life; the vision starts at the heart of the organization. Knowing that this is the reality, we feel it is imperative that every educator, in some way, shape, or form, must lead their space with heart—whether as a teacher in the classroom, or a principal of a school, or a superintendent of a district—the stories must come from the heart!

So, what does leading with the heart look like? What are the little tangible things that leaders with heart do on a regular basis? How does a leader with heart differ from the typical building leader? We acknowledge that we are not experts on the matter, and have no formal research that the ideas that we are about to share will actually work for everyone; however, because we love being instructional leaders and leading with our heart is all we know how to do (sometimes it can make things challenging), these are the little things that we do.

Here are ten tips from Tony that hopefully serve as a guide and resource for leading with heart, developing deep rooted connections with the community, and having a clear understanding of the stories that can be told.

1. I know the names of every one of our students; these children are so incredibly important to me and I feel that if I say hello to them by name whenever I pass them in the hallway, or sit next to them in their classroom, or play handball with them at recess,

they begin to understand that they are all very special to me! Our students, who are the most important members of this community, must know that their school is a safe haven where they can take risks, fail, and succeed. Our students must feel connected to their space because they are the voices that tell us if the brand experience matches the brand promise; our students must become the voices that tell the story!

2. I know as much as I can about each staff member and their lives beyond the school building (whatever they are comfortable sharing). As a parent, it is crystal clear to me that many of the things

Tips for Learning Student Names

1. Study the school yearbook.
2. Visit classrooms each day and focus on 2 to 3 kids in each class each day and keep repeating their names.
3. Focus on different grade levels each week.
4. Carry class lists with you as you walk the building and check off the names as you memorize them.

Tips for Nurturing Staff Connections

1. Spend 1:1 time with each staff member.
2. Listen more than you talk when engaging with staff.
3. Leave your door open so people can access you whenever they are ready to share.
4. Be as transparent as you can be about your life outside of school in order to establish trust.

that happen in my personal life directly shape and impact the decisions I make in my professional life and shape the stories I tell; by knowing my staff, on a somewhat personal level, I am better able to understand each person's perspectives, decisions, and needs, which are critical to the success of our school! For example, if one of our teachers gets a call from his or her child's school that their child is sick, then my priority becomes arranging coverage for that teacher to be able to leave immediately because that is where they are needed.

3. I announce the birthdays of each student and staff member during our daily morning announcements; I write a card for each staff member and invite each student down to my office to pick out a little birthday prize. Neither the cards nor the birthday prizes are a big deal (so glad that places like Oriental Trading exist), but I do believe they mean something to the people on the receiving end—they feel special; they feel acknowledged; they feel connected; and they want to be part of this story!

4. I am visible everyday to everyone (at least that is my goal until the administrative work gets in the way—but I limit that too, which I address). I am in the classrooms, the lunchroom, at recess, in the gym, and in the hallways all day. I literally avoid my office because I want to know what is going on in our school, in our classrooms, in the lives of our students and staff—how else can we shape and tell our stories if we are not living them? Although the school/district/classroom brand is not reliant on one person alone, the person leading the space certainly gives it life and influences its trajectory and therefore must be connected. By being connected to the daily happenings in our building, I am immediately able to communicate our successes to the community at large!

Tips for Being Visible

1. Block out time on your calendar each day for classroom observations and make sure your office staff know that this is sacred time.
2. Get to school early or stay late so you can finish the administrative tasks that do not involve other people.

5. I practice honest, clear, and consistent communications, which are critical keys to leading with heart! First, I write a weekly newsletter for the staff, *Fast Friday Focus*, where I spotlight all the amazing things

that happened in our school during that week. I spotlight different staff members each week and their varied instructional techniques and approaches because this type of sharing helps foster a professional learning community. It is not about someone being better than anyone else; it is about sharing information on great techniques, resources, and learning experiences because this knowledge helps us all grow! This weekly newsletter is critical because this is where the school brand begins to take shape—by everyone within the organization knowing what is happening in other rooms and learning spaces. By its very nature, our profession is isolating and in order to ensure that the school brand and story are consistent and reflective of what is happening throughout the organization, we must talk, collaborate, reflect, spotlight, and share. A sustainable brand is one that is built on a solid foundation that encompasses the entire community!

I also maintain this type of communication with the families of our children. Our district is now paperless, and 99 percent of our communication is via e-mail, so I e-mail the parents at least two to three times a week. At first, my e-mails weren't very "meaty"—for example, I spotlighted upcoming parent-teacher association (PTA) events, and schoolwide activities. As time went on, I realized that this regular e-mail correspondence to the parents (the Cantiague Daily Update) could be a powerful vehicle for spotlighting all the amazing things our kids were learning each day with their teachers—and these e-mails became my first attempt to tell our story and brand our school! As a parent, I know that when our son gets home from

> Thank you, Todd Whitaker, for the *Friday Focus* newsletter idea and many others that I learned from reading *What Great Principals Do Differently*—a must read for all instructional leaders!

school all he wants to talk about is lunch and recess—which is great, but I want to know what he is learning in math, what he is reading in class, or what he is creating in writing workshop. It is like pulling teeth to get him to talk about these subjects. So, my e-mails include details about all the upcoming events, but they also contain information about specific things our children are doing and learning at each grade level. By providing this information, I received a lot of feedback from the parents (which, in turn, led to the student-produced video updates, which I discuss later); many of them thanked me for sharing the specifics of the teaching and learning happening in our building because they are now able to engage their children about these experiences.

6. I try to bring people together on a regular basis. We are fortunate enough to have an auditorium in our school that holds about 450 people, and since our school has only about 400 kids, we are able to accommodate large gatherings. Although we don't have as many whole school assemblies as I would like, we schedule them periodically and they are critical to helping build community and fostering connections across grade levels!

Regarding my staff, I try to periodically host a few breakfasts and a luncheon throughout the year to bring everyone together in a comfortable and relaxed space. The daily pressures of being an educator, especially in this day and age, can be brutal, so coming together to just eat, chat, and laugh are crucial to sustaining the emotional well-being of each

> If you don't have an auditorium, you can use the gym or the field or even the front lawn— the location is not as important as the practice.

person in our building. These gatherings are the places where our school brand gets discussed, nurtured, and enhanced. These gatherings lead to the solidifying of our school vision, and our stories begin in these spaces!

7. I like to leave handwritten notes for our various staff members on a regular basis. The note may thank them for an amazing lesson, or for their efforts in helping a specific child, or for sharing with colleagues, or it may simply help put a smile on their face when things have been difficult. Whatever the goal or reason, a handwritten note goes a really long way! I try to write at least one note or card each week, but this practice is not always easy to

maintain. In an effort to save paper, I also recently started using the *Penultimate* app to e-mail "handwritten" notes to our teachers while I am in their classrooms, or right after. We are fortunate because our whole building was wired for WiFi two years ago, so I am able to use my iPad in many powerful ways!

8. I try to lead by example. For instance, I am really passionate about learning, teaching, and curriculum so I try to learn something new each day that I can share with our staff. Whether it is the reading and writing workshop models for literacy instruction, or the power of using *Twitter* for staff development, my goal is always to share what is current, powerful, and what can impact our children in the classrooms. I am always reading, learning, exploring, and doing because I want our school to be the best school on the planet for each child! Modeling and leading by example also ensure that the values and beliefs we espouse are clearly communicated to those around us and in turn help begin to shape our story.

9. I block out "observation" time in my calendar throughout the week, and I try to do all my administrative work (the paper pushing, e-mail sending, etc.) either early in the morning before school starts or late in the afternoon when the day is over and most people are gone. It is so important to be visible in the school community, and I feel strongly that the last place people should find me during the day is in my office. OK, so sometimes I "get in trouble" with colleagues or supervisors because I didn't respond to an e-mail fast enough (even though I do see every e-mail on my iPhone), or didn't return a phone call immediately, or am running late to a meeting, but the bottom line is that my kids and staff come first and the administrative stuff can wait, even just for a little while. (I know that being late to a meeting is not cool, so I am really working on that piece because I need to be respectful of other people's time.)

10. I love what I do! And we love what we do! Simply put, aside from our families, we live for being educators and instructional leaders and our passion for education is something we wear on our sleeves! We want to be a part of a team that creates a school that

any child, family, or staff member is proud to be a part of and whose stories always place the people (children, staff, and community members) at the center!

Well, we know that this list could go on and on. We know that there are a lot of other little things that we do in our daily work as leaders that are also really important, but we think that the above list, especially #10, outlines the main ingredients necessary to become a leader with *heart* each and every day! We are certain that many of you already practice these suggestions and more, because we believe that in order to be successful educators who can successfully brand their space, a lot of heart has to be injected into their daily work!

 CHAPTER 2—TWO TAKEAWAYS & A TIP

- Takeaway #1—Don't forget the ten steps to leading with heart: know the names of your students, know your staff, announce the birthdays of everyone in the school, be visible, maintain honest and consistent communication, bring the entire school community together as often as possible, leave handwritten notes for people, lead by example, block out time on your calendar to be in the classrooms, and love what you do.

- Takeaway #2—Although branding one's space relies heavily on matters of the mind, without a direct connection to the heart and soul of the organization, there is no real story to tell.

- Tip—Remember that a school vision starts at the core; the vision starts in the space that makes the organization tick; the vision starts in the traditions and values of the organization; the vision starts in the space that makes the organization breathe and come to life; the vision starts at the heart of the organization!

Building Your
Brand and Preparing
to Tell Your Story

T he real essence of building your brand begins with making a connection between your school and the public. Historically, schools relied on word of mouth and newsletters as their methods of communication to the public—that's right—TO the public; not WITH the public—there is a huge difference! Mind you, word of mouth and newsletters are useful, but neither are effective in isolation. The primary concern is that both forms are reactive, which means that there is no opportunity to be proactive. The communications are not happening in the moment, therefore the perception of the text or conversation can be swayed by the lack of consistency in delivery. Using those vehicles, it is a big risk to take if schools rely on the hope of those stories getting to the public. Telling the story of schools and districts allows you to create an accurate picture of exactly what is going on in your space, and helps to build social capital for when things are not going as you would like.

The development of social capital is something we don't talk enough about in schools. In general, schools are composed of people whose past experiences with education were positive and who were then motivated to get their teaching degrees, and come back to inspire the youth of tomorrow. Consider that the number of people who return to teach is incredibly small in comparison to the sum total of people who attended school. The reality is that not everyone had a great school experience. When our parents enter our schools and walk through the doors, it is important to understand that they may not see our environment as welcoming if they did not have positive experiences when they were students. Consequently, including the parents of students in the journey to build the brand and develop the identity of our schools can shift their perception of schools and a positive snowball effect can happen resulting in the growth of the number of advocates for your district and school.

The perception of public education has declined over the course of the last few years. The idea that incredible and positive things can happen in school settings is not discussed as much as one negative incident that happens on the playground, in the lunchroom, or on an athletic field. As you begin this process, the thought of building a brand in order to change the narrative of schools needs to be taken very seriously.

Joe's journey as a superintendent gives us insight into how the branding experience can begin. The first thought of building a brand came to our district when I was going through the interview process. The board was very proud of some things going on in the school, but the conversations they were having with community members revolved more around a single incident rather than encompassing the overall vision for the school district. During the interview process, they qualified the need for positive school promotion as a clear requirement for the superintendent position. The concept was easy . . . tell the story of the school. What we found was putting a plan in place to promote a consistent voice was paramount. Here are some important questions to consider when building your brand.

WHAT IS THE IDENTITY OF YOUR SCHOOL DISTRICT?

To truly start to build a brand you need to have an identity. A book can and has been written about how to develop that identity. The more your school district is connected with the process of developing the identity, the easier it is to disseminate to anyone outside of the building. The amount of people involved in spreading information about your image has a direct correlation to the number of people you have actively engaged in and out of the school district. If your identity is the best kept secret in town, you are not taking full advantage of the work done in your school. The positive push can come from anywhere, therefore involving the community in starting that journey is a significant way to develop social capital for your district—remember people, it is all about social capital!

CAN THE COMMUNITY AROUND YOU DESCRIBE YOUR IDENTITY?

The community wants to come along for the ride, if you give them the opportunity. When our elementary school developed the vision of "Fall Creek as a community that works, learns, and succeeds together," we involved the community by sending out the following notice on Facebook: *The first 5 people to find me at the football game and tell me the vision of Fall Creek Elementary will get a Go Crickets t-shirt!* The response was amazing. The first game produced kids of all sizes running up to me at the gate. The second game brought kids and adults of all sizes running up to me at the gate! Everyone loves school pride gear and using it to disperse the vision was a huge success, helping to ensure that the entire community—inside and outside of the school—were talking the same language and sharing a common vision.

IF YOU HAD ONLY 15 SECONDS TO TELL YOUR STORY, WHAT WOULD YOU SAY?

Call it an elevator speech or a commercial, whatever it is make sure it is consistent, clear, and to the point. Your community connects with people everywhere, at the grocery store, local food establishment, athletic events, school functions, parades, and so forth. Have the conversation start with what they saw on *Twitter, Instagram, YouTube,* or *Facebook* and help create a narrative that is so important to promote the district as opposed to what they heard about a student or some incident. At the start of every year, our teachers call parents and have a very quick, positive conversation about their child. The parent walks away with a good feeling about school since the first interaction is always positive. The same concept holds true with your school identity. If your community starts out with some positive information they saw online, people are smiling. First, the discussion starts in a positive manner. This is clearly important when people are talking about your school. Second, if one of the individuals in a discussion group is not an advocate for the school and someone else starts the conversation with a positive take on what is going on, the negative individual's audience shrinks. It's easy to pile onto a negative story, it's harder to start one. If there is no negative interaction to start, the conversation proceeds in favor of the district more often than not and the brand is nurtured and fostered in a healthy and positive way with the support and acceptance of the entire community.

WHAT IS THE MOST AMAZING THING ABOUT YOUR SCHOOL DISTRICT?

Some schools are STEM (science, technology, engineering, and mathematics) schools, magnet schools, 1:1 technology schools, performing arts schools, or whatever the current trends in public education.

Trying to develop a sense of identity is an important discussion to have with your district. There are times throughout the course of an implementation

> If the group can have a starting point that connects to something they have done successfully in the past, the likelihood of it succeeding grows exponentially.

phase when taking on a new initiative that people look around and think about all of the extra work. As a leader, connecting the new initiative to some program or system that is already in place in the school is one of the best ways to move the process forward.

One of the issues with new initiatives is the concern that it is just one more thing to put on the plates of our staff members. Unfortunately, there are teachers who determine the time left before their retirement by making comparisons to new initiatives rather than years . . ."Well, if I stick around for two more new buzz word initiatives, I can retire!" We are all human. If we see the value in an activity, we are more likely to engage in said activity because we own it, believe in it, and see the positive impact it has on kids and education. Conversely, if we don't see how a new initiative connects to what we are doing in the classroom or school, it is highly unlikely that we buy into the new process.

In building the brand process at your school, the most success comes from starting with the great things going on in your classrooms. In the first three days of school, all of our teachers make a positive parent call with a specific behavior that they observed and want to reinforce with students. The process of sending those messages out to the world does not change. There are amazing things happening in our building. Don't endorse the "what would I even send to parents" mentality. Have your staff write down one great thing going on in each of their classrooms and you now have a huge list of things to start communicating to the outside world.

CHAPTER 3—TWO TAKEAWAYS & A TIP

- Takeaway #1—A powerful exercise to consider when building your brand is asking yourself this question: If you only had 15 seconds to tell your story, what would you say? Have everyone in the organization or community reflect on this important question.

- Takeaway #2—When our families walk through the doors, we have to understand that they may not see our environment as welcoming if they did not have a good experience when they were students. Including them in the journey to build the brand and develop the identity can shift their perception of schools. When that perception is shifted, the positive snowball effect happens and the number of advocates for your district grows.

- Tip—Leave a "Notebook of Positive Experiences" by the sign-in book for parents to offer suggestions there. Share student stories and quotes from staff in your weekly updates.

CHAPTER

4

Using Social Media to Tell Your Story

G reat storytelling and great storytellers have the opportunity to rule the world. We use storytelling to connect to each other on different levels. When we were young, we wanted a story before we went to bed; when we were in school, we wanted the teacher to hear our story; and as adults we convene at restaurants, bars, and reunions to tell stories and revisit the times that made us the happiest. We all are selective about what we remember and our connections to the positive memories drive those conversations. The last minute wide-open jump shot to win the game in high school has turned into a recollection of a fadeaway, from the corner, over three people, from our knees. Even revisiting difficult times with your friends often results in reminiscences that made you better as a person, or helped you grow as a family or group. We thrive on storytelling and look for any opportunity to share our perspective.

We want to hear great stories. We want to invest in great stories. There is a reason why pregame shows before big events air mini-movies on members of the teams taking part in the contest. The network access to players, coaches, and families is unbelievable. Super Bowl coverage starts six hours before kickoff and is watched by an absurd number of people. We want to hear their stories. We want to connect with them, and because of that desire, programmers know that this is a way to attain higher ratings and boost exposure. When an Internet video goes viral, you often see talk show hosts and news stations lining up to interview those individuals involved and have them tell their story. We look for the story because we want to connect, and the emotion of the stories gives us that connection. To desire that connection is very human and derived from an emotional base.

The greatest stories in the world are real . . . and many of them are happening in our schools. Here is another piece of Joe's story: In Fall Creek, Wisconsin, there are over 800 stories everyday in our school—the melting pot of our public school system lends itself to the most incredible stories; however, the work that is done in classrooms, hallways, gyms, and auditoriums is often only shared with a select few. We hope for our kids to go home and tell the story of their school. We hope our families run into our teachers outside of school to have conversations about what happens in our schools. We hope a lot and hope is good, but the power of storytelling can't be left to hope. We need to promote the narrative that drives the great stories of kids.

We live in a true attention deficit society; must see TV is not a scheduled event anymore because all TV is now on our time. We can watch full seasons of shows, download podcasts, and aggregate stories in a publication that fit our needs . . . on our time. Take a look at someone as they check their phone for information. If something doesn't catch their eye right away, what happens? Their phone turns into a Roulette wheel and the emphatic scroll begins. Our stories have to grab the attention of the public and engage them in the wonderful things kids do in our school. In effect, we are storytelling through 140 characters, via an *Instagram* picture, or by a post on *Facebook*. We are using those vehicles to tell microstories in an effort to highlight the amazing work of kids. This also helps us build social capital with our stakeholders and invites them along for the ride called today's education.

Essentially, all of us can feel whatever we feel about the changes in society. We can blame the ills of the world on the idea that families no longer sit at a table and tell stories; and we can feel as if technology is taking over the world and people don't engage in meaningful conversations anymore. The reality is that meaningful conversations take place all the time—storytelling still occurs; it just happens in different ways and different times than before. I was on a *Voxer* conversation recently with seven of my true friends; yet, I have only met half of them in person. Our conversation lasted for hours, but actually took place in one or two minute blocks of time and on our schedules. We shared great stories in a medium that allowed us to connect when we could. Is this communication reality better or worse; I don't know. Is it different? Absolutely. For those who are unfamiliar, *Voxer* is a walkie-talkie multimedia-messaging app that allows you to have free verbal exchanges with individuals or groups of people in real time—it is similar to a live *Twitter* chat. It is a great way to connect with colleagues and create an ongoing conversation that works on your time schedule.

Families in our schools want to connect, but they want to do it on schedules that fit their timetables. There is nothing wrong with that—at the end of the day, it is not about the time of the connection, but whether or not the connection happens. We need to look at time as a commodity . . . one that we can harness, but not control. Parents and community members want to engage with us if we give them the opportunity, but do not force a time issue on them.

A picture, video, post, call, or text all can evoke profound emotions. Something impactful is always delivered when great stories touch our emotions; the world belongs to the storytellers. There are 800 people in this school, and they all have the desire to tell their stories and have their voices heard. If they don't have the medium, then the school should provide that opportunity. When we do, everyone has a chance to come along for the ride and become a part of the story and the storytelling.

Think back to when you were a kid. I brought home stuff from school that came out of the backpack and immediately was posted on the refrigerator. My mom used to display everything: draw a circle on a piece of paper . . . fridge; paint a line on construction paper . . . fridge; the one time I got 100 percent on a spelling test . . . fridge. As time went on, essays, my sister's grade reports, school pictures (fashion faux pas and mullets included) were all affixed on the central location in the kitchen. The place where everyone in the family went for nourishment was also the place they went to get an emotional pick-me-up. Many of the good things in our lives were prominently displayed in that place. Anyone who came to the house inevitably stopped at the fridge, and the displays sparked many conversations. The refrigerator, it turns out, was a great conduit to tell a story.

Social media has now brought the conversations that happened in kitchens everywhere to the masses. The pictures that used to be held by refrigerator magnets are now posted and shared through *Instagram*, *Twitter*, and *Facebook*. The opportunities to share data has grown exponentially. *Iphoto* streams can be shared with anyone and a story told through pictures. Obviously, these feeds and streams can become saturated over time, but the fact that our refrigerator was so covered in paper and pictures echoes the same concept. We *want* to share; we are *proud* of our kids and deep down we want others to know about their accomplishments.

Parents want to be connected and want to brag about what their kids are doing in school. They want to be proud of the school their children attend . . . who wouldn't?! There are a number of people following our district *Twitter* and *Facebook* feeds, but the real payoff comes when we review the feeds specific to our classrooms. Some of our teachers took the leap last year and helped parents sign up for *Twitter*. The teachers post often to keep families up to date on the great things going on in the classroom. They don't try to meet a quota of how many times they post or count to see which kids are in pictures . . . they just post . . . a lot. The feedback has been great! Essentially, families now have a running story of what happens in the classroom; and this practice is happening all over the country. Leaders like Ben Gilpin flood their *Twitter* feeds with the great things happening in their schools. Matt Gomez and Pernille Ripp are not only displaying what happens in their classrooms, but are allowing students to own the process through posts and blogs. The list clearly does not end there . . . hundreds of teachers across the country are connecting with their families through social media . . . but what if it was in the thousands . . . or more? When someone asks what is going on in your school, the evidence is right in your pocket . . . all the time. Stories can be shared with family, shown to coworkers, and provide a little smile when a day gets tough. Stories are told day in and day out in schools, and sharing those stories with the world is a great way to connect to families.

There will never be a time in education where someone walks into my office and says . . ."Wow, I just don't know what to do with all of this time." We expect a great deal from our group . . . and they deliver. Connecting with parents is simply not optional. How teachers connect with parents is based on comfort zone and time. As we move into an environment where the fridge has turned into a phone, it is essential to locate how parents live socially. *Twitter* and *Instagram* will inevitably turn into something else in a few years, and we will be ready. We want the conversations about what happens in our school to promote the positive things going on at every turn. The medium will change, but the commitment to creating opportunities for parents to connect to what we do will not. That commitment helps update the conversation that has occurred at kitchen tables since the dawn of time . . .

Parent: How was your day?

Student: Good.

Parent: What did you do?

Student: I don't know.

I used to live that discussion every day and now using social media as the new fridge swings that conversation. When kids own the process, when they know there is a connection to home and can take pride in what they do because they see it all the time, their response goes from "I don't know" to "I don't know where to start."

The process of telling your story is something that needs to be vetted into the framework of your school. Being too dependent on a particular vehicle for social media does not afford as much opportunity for change when the vehicle changes. Case in point: if we had invested all of our proverbial eggs in the *MySpace* basket, it would now be difficult to reach our intended audience. Having said that, there are tools that people are currently using that should help get you started. None of these tools are all inclusive, and that is OK. The connection to multiple tools helps reach different audiences. In the following paragraphs, we discuss some of these vehicles and how to connect so that the time invested is not as intense. Here are a few we use on a daily basis.

TWITTER

A socially networked online community, *Twitter* is one of the most popular social networking sites and is considered a form of microblogging that encourages educators to tweet and share their thoughts, opinions, and resources in 140 characters or less (Perez, 2012). *Twitter*, similar to other social networking sites like *Facebook* and *Instagram*, functions as a social learning resource and a space where educators can be exposed to different types of discourse and literacy practices (Greenhow, 2009). Learners can use *Twitter* to ask and answer each other's questions and, in turn, *Twitter* can help support collaboration and deeper understanding (Galagan, 2009).

When Osama bin Laden was captured and killed in Pakistan in 2011, the events of the raid began unfolding on *Twitter* before President Obama officially announced the news to the world on live television (Brenhouse, 2011). When Hurricane Sandy hit the

Northeast and ravaged New York City, the Jersey shore, and other areas on the East Coast, *Twitter* and other social media sites became a forum for crowd-sourced reporting featuring critical and actionable information about what was actually transpiring in real time (Oremus, 2012). Most recently, when Dr. John King, commissioner of education in New York State, decided to cancel a statewide "Town Hall" tour because the first meeting featured heated exchanges between members of the audience, the video of his reactions during that first meeting instantly went viral on *Twitter*. These examples touch on different subjects, but the connective thread is *Twitter* as a medium for establishing social connections with other people, and instantaneously sharing information and learning.

But, the power of *Twitter* does not stop there—it can easily become a platform for telling the story of your classroom, school, or district. Here are a few things to consider when planning to use *Twitter* to spread your story:

- Create an account and decide who is going to control it, have access to it, and be able to tweet; one way to go is to create a classroom, school, or district account.

- Decide if your account will be locked (you must authorize followers) or unlocked (anyone can follow you). There may be a districtwide policy or practice so check before making this decision.

- Discuss content—what types of things can be tweeted (what types of pictures, what text should be included, etc.).

- Inform and educate the community—it is imperative that families understand how *Twitter* is being used and how they can join, follow, and become part of the conversation.

- Pick a hashtag (#gocrickets and #Cantiague are our hashtags) and use them in every tweet you send—this helps build your brand and allows people to follow your story with ease.

- Connect with other passionate and dedicated educators to create and build your professional/personal learning network (PLN) because they will offer amazing ideas that can be personalized for your space and help to contribute to your brand.

- Model for your staff and kids . . . . Model, model, model! If those around us see how we are using a platform like *Twitter*, we help lower their anxiety, help demystify the negative connotations, and help them understand how we harness this medium to tell our collective stories. Here is a look into Tony's daily world as it relates to his *Twitter* use: I walk around school with my iPad mini in hand and spend hours visiting classrooms and capturing images of what is happening. Then, I make it my goal to explain the *how* and *why* behind every image so that we are completely transparent with the community. We want them to know all the awesome things happening in our school and we want them to know now! As of today, two thirds of the classrooms at Cantiague are actively tweeting and I also involve the children in the *Twitter* experience. For example, recently I was in a third-grade classroom and took some pictures of the children engaged in their independent reading time. One of the pictures really intrigued me and was of a boy reading on his iPad; I was having a difficult time captioning the picture, so I decided to include the student in that process. So, together, we discussed the picture and we generated a caption together—actually, he generated it mostly on his own. He was able to explain the *how* and *why* of the picture in less than 140 characters. In my mind, that speaks to college and career readiness much more powerfully than any score on a multiple-choice test. What better way to illustrate student voice when telling your school story—not only did this little guy tell his story, but I was also able to model appropriate digital citizenship for him by going through the process step by step. That is why modeling is critical in the branding experience!

FACEBOOK

Facebook continues to be the monster of all social media sites. Though it may be replaced with something in the future, it is an ideal vehicle for school communications. With 128 million daily users in the United States, Facebook still has the largest reach in the social media world (Smith, 2014). The dynamics of *Facebook* are interesting. The majority of *Facebook* users are in the 18 to 35 age category. Over the course of the last three years, *Facebook* users from the ages of 13 to 17 have dropped 25 percent and the number of users aged 55 and over has increased by 80 percent (Saul, 2014). This trend tells us that teens are leaving for new media, parents live in this space, and grandparents are jumping on to connect at incredible rates. If you are looking to only connect with parents, alumni, and grandparents, then *Facebook* is the correct medium to use. However, if you are looking to connect with students, a new space needs to be explored.

REMIND

Remind (formerly *Remind 101*) is a great tool to communicate with students and families who are not connected to social media outlets or just want another vehicle for information. *Remind* is a text messaging service that teachers can use to text students from a computer or mobile device for free without collecting students' cell phone numbers. It is essentially a single-user operation, which means that students are unable to text back to the teacher, but it is great for communication of events, assignments, and school emergency information. It is free to sign up, and the organizer (teacher or school) is the only one who needs an account. Parents can sign up via text or e-mail so it works on a number of different devices. You can add up to ten classes or groups to the account. From a school district perspective, this is very useful if you want one person to control multiple accounts for different buildings. Athletic teams, clubs, and classes are ideal candidates to use *Remind* and can clearly take advantage of this medium.

YOUTUBE, IPAD VIDEOS, OTHER VIDEO TOOLS

There are many ways to use videos to tell your story and build your brand! At Cantiague, this year we started a new activity called weekly video updates where six or seven students from each class conduct research about activities and events that are happening at each grade level and then they share those updates on camera. The children are allotted two days for their grade-level research, then they join me for lunch on Wednesday or Thursday and we make the video. The children make the best storytellers and who better to share what's happening in our schools than the people who are experiencing it firsthand—our amazing kids! That is the power of student voice (#StuVoice).

Here are some helpful video hints based on our experiences at Cantiague.

- Use whatever video platform that works best for you. We use the *Touchcast* app (see below for more details) on my iPad, which is free and allows for 5-minute videos. This app also gives you the option to add in sound effects, pictures on the screen, and other video enhancing features.

- After creating the video, we upload it to our *YouTube* channel. Although a *YouTube* channel is not a necessity, it does provide an online space to house your videos and allows for easy sharing with the entire community via an e-mailed link— again, not a must, but something to consider. The great thing about *YouTube* is that it is linked to *Google* so that you can set your channel as public or private, which is definitely important for the community to understand.

- Once the video is posted on *YouTube*, we e-mail the link out to our families and share it on *Twitter* to get as many people to watch it as possible! At this point, our weekly video updates have been featured in presentations by different educators around the world; as a result, our children literally have a global audience. That is another layer to the power of using social media to tell your story—people from around the world can hear your students tell your story—that is the power in flattening the walls to your school, your classroom, and your district by taking the time to tell your story and beginning to brand your space!

TOUCHCAST APP, WEB-BASED RESOURCES

Sorting through the abundance of video making apps, screencasting apps, and web-based resources, our school's app of choice is *Touchcast*. The app is free to download on an iPad and also has a web-based feature. Just establish an account and you are ready to start creating your own video updates for your community. Why do we recommend *Touchcast*? Well, here are some of its great features:

- It is free and you can create up to 5-minute videos (any longer and most people tune out).
- It allows you to merge multiple videos into one final product.
- You can easily flip the camera so that you can record from either side of the device if you are using an iPad.
- You can add sound effects—laughter, applause—to any video production; just remember to end the sound effect before you start talking, otherwise your voice is lost.
- There is a whiteboard feature on the app so that you can write things during the video—the whiteboard can look like a traditional whiteboard or can even look like glass.
- There is a teleprompter feature, which is awesome when working with little kids who might not remember what they want to say during the video.
- There are different themes incorporated so that the screen can look like a news channel or a sports channel—great way to personalize the product.
- There is a green screen feature and if you have a green wall, you can add all sorts of graphics, pictures, or images right there during the video.
- You can add a screen within the screen where you can feature someone in the video, or pictures, other videos, your *Facebook* page, your *Twitter* feed, a link to a website or even a *Google* map—the possibilities are endless. This is a powerful way to personalize your story even further.

- It is super easy to use, and you can easily turn it over to your students so that they can produce and direct the videos!

BLOGS

Blogs, whether they are classroom-based, schoolwide, or districtwide, are another powerful way to create your brand and communicate your story. Blogs are a great option for reflecting on all the *hows* and *whys* unfolding within our schools; they are also a nice platform for sharing pictures and videos with the community. Two of the most popular free blogging sites are *Blogger* (through *Google*) and *WordPress*. Both of these platforms have apps that can be accessed on a smartphone or tablet and help facilitate the blogging experience.

A blog, which can be updated easily and regularly, is one platform available to educators to share their stories and build their brands. If this is the instrument you elect, establish a format or template that works for you and then regularly update it. For example, at Cantiague I use a blog to create a weekly staff newsletter because I think it is a critical way to ensure that the brand promise is matching the brand experience! In our newsletter, I share typical administrative odds and ends, but I also take the opportunity to spotlight three amazing things that happened during that week in the building. In that manner, the staff automatically can see the awesome things happening in the building and the important steps that contribute to creating our school brand—specifically, what we consider important and why. By allowing the staff insight into each other's works and successes, we not only ignite collaboration, but the message is clear about what is valued and what is viewed as core to our school brand. If it is being spotlighted in the newsletter, it is valued and should be replicated in other spaces!

A couple of tips before you actually go to set up a school, or district, or classroom blog.

- Think long and hard about the name of the blog. It doesn't sound that important, but the name is critical because it feeds directly into the school identification and brand!

- Decide on a format, template, or layout you prefer by visiting and exploring other blogs—this is so important.

- Embed your *Twitter* feed, pictures, and other important links into your blog as they directly connect to your brand and help further tell your story.

- Make sure that you clear the class blog with administration before using it . . . unless you are one of those people who ask for forgiveness before permission . . . then just go for it!

VIRTUAL NEWSLETTERS, SMORES, WEEBLY

Not certain if you are ready to use social media to tell your story? Do you enjoy the more traditional newsletter approach? Then you may want to consider one of the following options for your community story:

- E-mail your newsletter so the news gets delivered in a timely fashion. Write the newsletter in the traditional way if that feels more comfortable and then copy and paste it into the body of an e-mail. By using e-mail, the information gets out to parents in a more timely and current fashion—they can talk to their children about what just happened instead of what happened weeks ago. You may want to consider sending a shorter, more frequent e-mail newsletter to raise the levels of family engagement, which is always the goal when telling our story and building our brand.

- *Smore*—go to www.smore.com and create your own newsletter or flyer! This web-based site offers templates that a school or district can drop into text, videos, and pictures to share stories with the community. With a few clicks of the button, you can create a sharp and clean newsletter to share with families via e-mail and accessed on a computer, tablet, or smartphone—remember, most of our families have access to at least one of those devices.

- *Glogster*—this web-based resource at www.glogster.com is similar to *Smore* in that you can drop in text, pictures, and videos of all the amazing things happening in your school and then share them with the entire community with the click of a button via e-mail. One of the best things about tools such as *Smore* and *Glogster* is that you can create a student group or club that is assigned the responsibility for generating the entire piece—they decide what gets featured, included, and spotlighted! This is such a powerful and easy way to put student voice at the center of your storytelling!

SCHOOL DISTRICT APP

The development of a district app affords you the opportunity to provide a "one stop shop" for everyone with access to a smartphone. According to Business Insider (a leading online business news site), 78 percent of the adult population (ages 15 to 64) use smartphones (Blodget, 2013). Frequently, we are asked what we are doing for those people in the community without access to technology (we address this later in the chapter), but if we currently have the ability to reach 80 percent of our population within that age group with a specific vehicle, we think taking advantage of that opportunity is essential. The U.S. Census Bureau released some statistics in 2013 that indicated 81 percent of families in poverty owned a cell phone. The percentage of families in poverty using smartphones has increased over the last two years as well. Forbes projects that 87 percent of connected device subscriptions sold by 2017 will be for smartphones and mobile tablets (Columbus, 2013). The smartphone with data plan may be a less expensive option than phone or cable company Internet service and may be one of the reasons for the increased use by the lower socioeconomic subgroup. Accordingly, the use of a smartphone app can be extremely advantageous for students, teachers, parents, and community members. The app that we use for our district provides the following items through the interface: top stories from the district, daily announcements, a district calendar, school menus, a staff directory, newsletters, student information access, a superintendent blog, a district live stream channel, a tip line to connect with district leadership, and access to *Instagram*, *Flickr*, *Twitter*, *Facebook*, and *Youtube*. It affords a channel where everyone can go to get any information needed regarding school district communications. It has been extremely successful in our district. In the initial 10 months of access, our school district had over 500 downloads of the app; a number that is very telling in a school district composed of 800 students. The school continues to push information to this area and hopes that it grows in popularity. As indicated by survey data, within the app the most popular features are the calendar and social media connections. The calendar allows users to download events directly to their own devices, and the social media connections allow them to see what is going on in that space without having to open an account. The development of our app was contracted through an outside provider, but there are also opportunities to construct a similar app in-house through development apps, such as *Conduit Mobile*. Another option is to have a few interested students develop the app for the school. As interfaces for developers get easier to use, more and more people will begin to develop their own. At this point in the process, my school was willing to spend a small portion of our budget to have someone develop a professional quality app that was easy to use.

POSTING TO MULTIPLE AREAS—TIPS AND TRICKS

"It's easy for you because you are technologically savvy." We get this comment a lot, but in truth it has less to do with being technologically savvy and more to do with finding ways to tell our story. The cumulative amount of time we spend connecting the story of our classrooms to the public is not enormous; it just seems that way because we are connecting using multiple platforms throughout the course of the day. Here are a few ways to connect multiple accounts so that it is not an arduous task.

Third-Party Apps to Connect Platforms

There are a number of different third-party apps that allow posting to multiple platforms at one time. In these formats, you can select the social media site you wish to use and then post to those areas.

At our school, we use *Twitter* and *Facebook* more than any other area so that when posts are developed they can be updated and sent directly to those two sites without an extra step. One word of caution when using these apps is to remember the character count. *Facebook* allows you to use as many characters as you want in a post. *Twitter* only allows 140 characters, therefore if you are attempting to post information to both sites, review the character count, otherwise your post will only go to *Facebook*. One of the real advantages to using *HootSuite* (a social media management system) is the opportunity to schedule tweets and posts. Future dates (i.e., parent-teacher conferences, scheduled days off, spirit day, school pictures, etc.) can all be scheduled to tweet or post out the day before or the day of an event as a reminder. This way if you are busy prior to an event, you know that you already have the tweet or post ready to relay.

Automatic Posts

Accessing the website *www.facebook.com/twitter* allows you to connect your *Facebook* at *Twitter* accounts so that when a post is updated through your *Facebook* account, it automatically updates your *Twitter* feed. This is very handy if you use both media, but realize that there is a drawback. If you choose to go this route, the posts to *Twitter* are not native, which means that any link takes the user to the connected *Facebook* page. Essentially, any post that goes beyond the 140-character limit links to the *Facebook* page. This is not necessarily an excluding option, but if you intend to post pictures or links, it is easier to view them through your *Facebook* page.

Instagram

Instagram is an online photo and video sharing platform that allows users to take pictures and send them directly to other social networking sites. The unique features of *Instagram* are that the photos are square-shaped and short videos can be added to your feed. *Instagram* has an option before a picture is posted to your account to request whether you want to send an update to *Facebook*, *Twitter*, *Flickr*, and *Tumblr*. By connecting your accounts in the settings tab, it is really easy to share to all of the sites with just a few clicks. Our school uses *Instagram* as a vehicle to get pictures to other social media sites and recognize a significant number of followers attracted to this vehicle. In our particular area, middle school students are now the highest number of *Instagram* users. The increased practice of employing mobile devices in schools has enhanced the *Instagram* experience, and it can be a great way for staff to connect project work and communication with learners.

Storify

What do we do for all the families who are still uncertain about delving into the world of social media? Well, fortunately, there is *Storify*, which is a web-based (and app-based) resource that facilitates gathering posts from different social media platforms (e.g., *Twitter*, *Facebook*, *Instagram*, etc.) and pulls all that information together within one link that can be e-mailed out to the entire community. This platform gives the community access to all the texts and pictures in one streamlined presentation that may have previously been shared in another format. Check out their website at www.storify.com.

With the speed of technology, it is a given that all of these platforms eventually will be replaced or adjusted in the future. They may be very popular for a particular amount of time and then be replaced by something newer, faster, more intuitive, and easier to use. Though the platforms change, the process should not. The business of building the identity of your brand and telling the story of your kids using an ever-changing world of communication demands flexibility. If you are committed to that identity and the importance of telling student stories, then the inevitable change in platforms will not and should not inhibit your drive to promote the great things happening in your school.

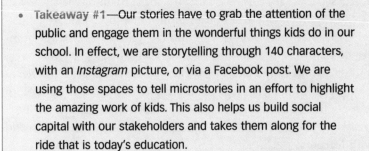

💿 CHAPTER 4—TWO TAKEAWAYS & A TIP 💿

- Takeaway #1—Our stories have to grab the attention of the public and engage them in the wonderful things kids do in our school. In effect, we are storytelling through 140 characters, with an *Instagram* picture, or via a Facebook post. We are using those spaces to tell microstories in an effort to highlight the amazing work of kids. This also helps us build social capital with our stakeholders and takes them along for the ride that is today's education.

- Takeaway #2—Some of the tech-based resources to consider when starting to brand your space and tell your story include *Twitter*, *Instagram*, *Facebook*, a blog, a video update featuring students and staff, a virtual newsletter, or even creating your own app.

- Tip—Using whatever resource you are most comfortable with, start small and build from there—diving into the deep end of the pool and trying out multiple resources at the same time can be quite overwhelming.

Giving Voice to All Stakeholders in the Storytelling Experience

When something goes viral, or becomes popular through the process of sharing on social networking sites, it is because the capacity to push the content was established. Content cannot go viral if only one person shares it with friends and then the process stops. Often we find only a few people in charge of the social media sites in school districts. The sharing of content is often left to a few individuals with knowledge of the process; there are a few reasons why this happens in schools.

School Internet safety poses a clear roadblock to opening the gates of information to the general public. School districts have a responsibility to keep kids safe during the day. Safety is both a physical and emotional state of being, so opening the network to everyone can cause a great deal of understandable fear to the school district administration and boards. Having said that, students are smart and find ways to bypass firewalls. Our experience is that students access sites with educational value more often than sites that might be considered inappropriate. We also live in a technological era where they do not need to log-in to the district server to retrieve desired data. Cellular access is fast enough for students to access any data they need outside of the WiFi in the school. This fact requires that schools examine the idea of what they can and cannot lock down. We still block certain sites at different grade levels to protect the students, but we do need to trust that kids will take responsibility and use the school network in the correct manner. Trust is a huge component when it comes to who should be allowed access to district accounts. It can definitely cause unsettling feelings to turn over the account to a student knowing that whatever is typed can't be revoked and might cause trouble for those who see it or read it. Setting up parameters for everyone who accesses the account and developing a strong knowledge of digital citizenship goes a long way to ease the fears associated with this process.

Student and staff ownership can also be a roadblock in the process. Students love the idea of social media, but are not always keen on letting other people access their world. They have no issue with friends, and sometimes friends of friends, having access to their world, but when it comes to an educator being one click away from an *Instagram* picture or tweet, they don't feel the same way. This reluctance can clearly inhibit students from being part of the process.

Creating capacity to build the brand of your school is truly vital to spreading the word about the great things kids are doing in and out of the building. Allowing students to control district accounts sounds like a risky proposition; too often we fear what might happen and then make decisions based on what a small population of our student staff may do. In reality, we should be making decisions based on our best students. If we set up policy and procedures to address misbehavior, we can certainly trust the process and allow another opportunity for student voice. Though the majority of school districts still don't want to allow students to directly provide content through district approved accounts, some districts have realized incredible success by handing the reins to students.

In Fall Creek, classroom *Twitter* accounts are downloaded onto devices used in the classroom and students tweet from that account periodically throughout the year. At the beginning of the process, teachers go through what a tweet is, why we would tweet, and the logistics of getting their thoughts out to the world. Individual students take over the account during scheduled events and live tweet to share the story of the classroom. They start their journey into digital citizenship and, early on, have the conversation about what it means to be part of the global network. Throughout the day, you can find students saying, "Hey, we should tweet that," and they are given that opportunity throughout the school year. This empowers the class to take pride in their work, knowing that their work goes beyond the walls of the school. This concept has grown and multiple classrooms now are participating in *Twitter* as a way to share their experiences. At the beginning of the school year, we set up computers in the classrooms for parents to sign up for *Twitter* if they elected. This year, students taught their parents how to sign up, follow great people, and even send out their first tweet. As a school, the #gocrickets hashtag is added to posts from kindergarten through high school and parents can follow along from their *Twitter* account or from the front page of the website. At Cantiague Elementary, we use the hashtag #Cantiague in every tweet we send, and at this point, more than half the staff is tweeting on a regular basis; the children have become an integral part of the experience as well by taking pictures and generating the accompanying captions for the tweet.

In Shullsburg, Wisconsin, Principal Melissa Emler gave the responsibility of their school district's social presence to the students. She has three social media interns who are in charge of the school's *Facebook*, *Twitter*, and *Instagram* accounts. They started the #shullsburgpride hashtag and promote it on a regular basis. Their work did not always resonate with their peers. In discussing the process with the current interns, they indicated that the idea of sharing what is going on in the school started very slowly. Posting scores from games and a few pictures on *Facebook* has turned into an increased reach in multiple platforms to meet the needs of their community. They are responsible for analyzing the data to see what posts have done well and for developing a plan for the best way to share their story. Mrs. Emler and her students also developed a social media class which starts in the fall at their high school. The syllabus can be found by visiting the Shullsburg School District home page. They are doing amazing things, and look forward to reaping the personal and school benefits from their hard work.

In Franklin Park, Illinois, Principal Jason Markey and the Leyden High School crew have set a new standard when it comes to student voice in telling the story of their school. They believe that the story is the school's to tell and have made their brand visible to everyone possible. They use the hashtag #leydenpride to promote the great things in their school. By promoting the hashtag, they are not locked into a few people controlling the message, but trust the group to inspire each other through the communication. Students, parents, staff members, community members, and local media have all shared information using the hashtag. Utilizing a common hashtag also affords them the opportunity to have alumni involved in sharing the great story of students. Their entries are in real time and crowdsourced to tell the story directly. They don't need to wait until a newsletter comes out to bring the great events to life. They have also started a #leydenpride scholarship that promotes what is great about Leyden High School beyond the walls of their school. Recently, they brought back a dance that had gone away for a few years; its resurgence was singularly due to a movement on *Twitter* to bring it back. The event was deemed "The Dance that Twitter Built." Each week a different student is given the school *Twitter* account and then posts his or her experiences to the site. This allows the school to promote and take pride in the school activities as presented from many different perspectives. According to Mr. Markey, students have been incredibly receptive and responsible in their efforts to tell the story of #leydenpride.

Just outside of Madison, Wisconsin, Pernille Ripp, one of our Connected Educators, has her students contributing to the world through blogging. Students write numerous posts throughout the year about their experiences in her fifth-grade classroom. Pernille uses her contacts as an author and blogger to help her students understand the power of connecting. The ownership of the process that they receive by their inclusion helps them to understand what unbelievable stories they have to tell. Their voices are reflected in the diversity of the themes of the blogs, which range from school assignments to true passion projects. Pernille takes pride in assisting every student with the understanding that each has such a unique voice, and the world needs to hear it. The excitement that comes from others reading and commenting on their blogs is enough to motivate them to contribute to the world. They also comment on the blogs of their classmates. As opposed to contributing dead-end comments, the students actively discuss the importance of continuing the conversations by asking questions and creating connections as opposed to adding comments like "nice blog post," in effect, stopping the conversation. They are taught to contribute, reflect, and question . . . all in a space that is safe, but public. It is the actual world of our kids, and Pernille is affording her students a platform for their voices that has impact well beyond their time in her classroom.

In Texas, Matt Gomez (@edcampDallas founder and #kinderchat moderator) starts the year discussing the impact of social media with his class. They are in kindergarten! They use Skype to have a conversation with a staff member in the building. When it is over, they walk to the staff member's room or area so that these 5-year-old children understand that there was a real person on the other side of the screen. They have the conversation about connecting, and that is the beginning of a fantastic journey into telling their stories. Throughout the year, these kids post pictures, videos, and messages from their classroom. Families have the opportunity to connect with the class on a daily basis, and these kindergarten kids see and learn the power of social media and the connection to the outside world. The transparency in the classroom clearly helps Matt develop trust with the parents in his room, and the students get an early indication of the digital footprint they are able to control in this world.

These are just a few examples of the wonderful things happening across the country. There are so many stories, but the best ones come from those educators willing to allow students to access their voice and promote the great things happening in their schools. If we allow students to own the process, they begin to identify with the schools, and their connectivity opens the doors to incredible ownership of the school community.

 CHAPTER 5—TWO TAKEAWAYS & A TIP

- **Takeaway #1**—When beginning your branding process, think about a hashtag that reflects your space and that can be used in multiple platforms to tell your story. Consider the hashtags spotlighted in this chapter: #gocrickets #Cantiague #leydenpride or #shullsburgpride. Pick one that works best for your space, but whatever you choose remember one thing— keep it short and make it memorable.

- **Takeaway #2**—Be certain to create capacity to build the brand of your school as this is truly vital to spreading the stories of the great things kids are doing in and out of the building.

- **Tip**—Consider giving students the power of controlling the school or district social media accounts, or contributing to them with the help of staff members. Let them be the voice that tells the school story. Don't forget to teach digital citizenship; the students live in this space and we need to educate them to use it effectively.

CHAPTER
6

Does the Brand Promise Match the Brand Experience?

Before you actually dive into the process of how to brand your school and the ways that you decide to tell your story, we are going to reiterate the questions we first posed in the introduction to this book. Only now, we want you to be certain of the answers:

- Does the brand promise of our school or district match our brand experience?

- What is our story? What do I believe in? What do I stand for? What do I want for our students and staff?

- If our staff was asked the questions above, would they answer them the same way that I did?

- If our students were asked the questions above, would their responses match my answers?
- If our community was asked the above questions, would they answer in the same way?

These questions and their answers are at the root of your brand and must be communicated clearly when you begin telling your story. This journey should start within the walls of the school between the leadership and staff. Work should be devoted to discussing and reflecting on what the school believes in and stands for as it relates to the students, the instruction, and a basic philosophy. If all the adults in the school are on the same page, then it is time to spread that message to the students and community members. It is imperative that whatever you say is happening in your school is actually happening in the classrooms, lunchroom, and even at recess. There must be pictures, words, and other forms of "evidence" gathered that support the brand promise you make to the community so that it seamlessly aligns to the actual experiences that children are having . . . the brand experience.

From Tony's perspective, here is a concrete example from Cantiague Elementary that breaks down how the brand promise matches the brand experience. When I think about our brand promise as compared to our brand experience, I can confidently say that the two are closely aligned. For example, we promise to meet the needs of each child regardless of readiness levels and abilities. Based on conversations held with different family and staff members about this promise to our student body, almost everyone comments on our ability to differentiate instruction to meet the needs of individual students. The idea of differentiating instruction also serves as a springboard for the way we instruct children in general. Our community knows we believe in using small group instruction as much as possible and that whole class direct instruction is at a minimum. By working with children in small groups, we can heighten proximity and impact student engagement in positive ways. We spotlight these ideas and practices through our book clubs, guided reading lessons, small group math activities, and group research projects.

Additionally, our community knows that we believe in reading and writing workshop models as the anchor of our literacy instruction. The workshop model is rooted in the gradual release of responsibility for learning from the teacher to the student. The teacher begins by modeling a skill, then the children try it with some support, and eventually the children employ the strategy during their independent work time. We embrace this approach because two of our goals are to nurture lifelong readers and to support passionate authors who cannot wait to publish their original works.

Our community also knows that the social, emotional, and psychological development of our children is as much a priority as the academic development of our students. We employ a full-time school psychologist to work with children at all grade levels to assist in the development of social skills, to help students problem solve, and to support the students as they develop and internalize the skills necessary to be mindful with their actions. Furthermore, our community knows that we are "bucket fillers" in our school (a program that teaches children the value of their words and actions), and that we support the Super Six—Be a Superstar program designed to promote responsible, respectful, positive, safe, and kind kids: these programs are the pillars of our success. In order to align the experience with the promise, we implemented a positive behavior referral system in the school where teachers share notes with me about something a student did that qualifies him or her as a future bucket filler. I telephone to share the great news with the parents and then later in the week that same student is recognized as "Bucket Filler of the Week" and is featured on our website (important storytelling on a personal level). We believe in the philosophy behind the Bucket Filling program; as a result our students and community completely embrace it, and the corresponding verbiage we use in school is regularly heard in the community. From my perspective, this is where we have done the best job of aligning the brand promise with the brand experience. In the end, our community knows that we love our kids and are dedicated not only to their academic development, but also to their social, emotional, and psychological growth.

I share this information in order to explain the conscious decision I made to promote our school brand and to tell our story; this decision changed the tone in the entire building. I have witnessed the conversations at our parent-teacher association (PTA) meetings evolve from talking about the logistics of fundraisers, to discussing the concerns over high-stakes testing, to the power of book clubs as a way to differentiate instruction because we branded ourselves as a school that does not place value on these tests, but proudly supports book clubs. Our community is informed, and that is what we want at Cantiague. It means that we have to be transparent in both the brand promise and brand experience, which is why we rely on *Twitter* to show the reality. What does that mean? It means that we have to be confident in our choices. It means that we have to be open to feedback—good and bad. It means that we have to show that with every success, there are at least three failures. It means that we are comfortable flattening the walls of our school and proud of the brand we are marketing. In the end, when we give families insight into *how* and *why* we do things (which is central to branding and telling one's story), we switch gears from family involvement to true family engagement.

These are just some examples of how the brand promise matches the brand experience at Cantiague. I am sure that all of you can think of ways where that alignment is clear in your classrooms, schools, and districts—so, that is where you begin to build your brand and answer the question about whether the brand experience matches the brand promise!

 CHAPTER 6—TWO TAKEAWAYS & A TIP

- Takeaway #1—Ask yourself whether the brand promise matches the brand experience. That alignment is fundamental to a successful brand because if the two do not align, the brand will crash and burn.

- **Takeaway #2**—Work should be devoted to discussing and reflecting about what the school believes in and stands for as it relates to students, instruction, and philosophy. If all the adults in the school are on the same page, then it is time to spread that message to the students and community members. It is imperative that whatever you say is happening in your school is actually happening in the classrooms, lunchroom, and even at recess!

- **Tip**—Use the guiding questions at the start of this chapter as a resource for meetings with students, staff, and parents. For example, during your next PTA meeting, throw out some of those questions and see what answers people generate—it can be a powerful (potentially scary) experience.

CHAPTER
7

It's a Wrap

School should be about educating all kids. Every child who enters our schools has a story to tell regardless of ability, background knowledge, or socioeconomic level. Some have the ability to tell their own stories, some do not, but all deserve to have their voices heard. As administrators, we often defer to outside voices to define our schools based on a past history and negative experiences. The schools have the power and opportunity to shift the mind-set of those in the public sector—if we shout out and air the positive experiences and great accomplishments of our kids in our schools. When the proverbial dust settles, in the final analysis the only narrative of consequence within our classrooms, in the schools, and in the districts is the narrative about the children. It has to be about the kids . . . every single one of our kids. We do this for every one of the kids who walks through our doors regardless of language, ethnicity, or gender. We owe it to them—not because it is our job, or because someone did it for us, or even because these kids will be taking care of us someday—we owe it to them because they deserve the best. They deserve to have a voice in the educational experience. They deserve to be at the center of the stories.

No questions . . . they come to us as innocent 4-year-olds and trust that we will help make them better. They test our patience and as educators we spend the majority of our professional lives with our happiness determined by the attitudes and actions of children between the ages of four to eighteen. Having said that, we chose this extraordinarily important career path and the children deserve everything we can do to make their time with us magical. Telling the story of that journey is something they will not forget—nor will you! No matter where you go from here, never give up the opportunity to say something great about your classroom, school, or district. Now, get out there and build your brand and tell your unique story!

 CHAPTER 7—TWO TAKEAWAYS & A TIP

- Takeaway #1—We have the power and opportunity to shift the mind-set of those in the public sector if we shout out via social media the great things that kids do in our schools.

- Takeaway #2—No matter where you go from here, never give up the opportunity to say something great about your classroom, school, or district.

- Tip—Get out there! Start building your brand and telling your story.

References

Blodget, H. (2013). Actually, the U.S. smartphone revolution has entered the late innings. *Business Insider*. Retrieved from http://www.busines sinsider.com/us-smartphone-market-2012-9#ixzz37qUQIb2b

Brenhouse, H. (2011). Man live-tweets U.S. raid on Osama bin Laden without knowing it. *Time Magazine*. Retrieved from http://newsfeed.time .com/2011/05/02/man-live-tweets-u-s-raid-on-osama-bin-laden-with out-knowing-it/

Columbus, L. (2013). IDC: 87% of connected devices sales by 2017 will be tablets and smartphones. *Forbes*. Retrieved from http://www.forbes .com/sites/louiscolumbus/2013/09/12/idc-87-of-connected-devices-by-2017-will-be-tablets-and-smartphones/

Galagan, P. (2009). Twitter as a learning tool. Really. *T + D, 63*(3), 28–29, 31.

Greenhow, C. (2009). Tapping the wealth of social networks for professional development. *Learning & Leading with Technology, 36*(8), 10–11.

Henderson, A. T., & Mapp, K. L. (2002). *A new wave of evidence: The impact of school, family, and community connections on student achievement (Annual Synthesis)*. Austin, TX: National Center for Family and Community Connections with Schools and SEDL.

Oremus, W. (2012). You're not a detective, but you play one on the Internet. *Slate Magazine*. Retrieved from http://www.slate.com/blogs/future_tense/2012/12/14/sandy_hook_elementary_shooting_why_we_rushed_to_find_adam_and_ryan_lanza.html

Perez, L. (2012). Innovative professional development: Expanding your professional learning network. *Knowledge Quest, 40*(3), 20–22.

Saul, D. J. (2014). *3 million teens leave Facebook in 3 years: The 2014 Facebook demographic report*. Retrieved from http://istrategylabs.com/2014/01/3-million-teens-leave-facebook-in-3-years-the-2014-facebook-demo graphic-report/

Smith, C. (2014). *By the numbers: 125 amazing Facebook user statistics*. Retrieved from http://expandedramblings.com/index.php/by-the-numbers-17-amazing-facebook-stats/#.UxtqEuddWrc

A SAGE Company

Corwin is committed to improving education for all learners by publishing books and other professional development resources for those serving the field of PreK–12 education. By providing practical, hands-on materials, Corwin continues to carry out the promise of its motto: **"Helping Educators Do Their Work Better."**

DATE DUE

PRINTED IN U.S.A.